WineStyle

PASO ROBLES WINE COUNTRY
SAN LUIS OBISPO WINE COUNTRY

BAY PUBLISHING COMPANY
MONTEREY, CALIFORNIA

ISBN 0-9742147-2-8

Published by Bay Publishing Company
395 Del Monte Center, #103
Monterey, California 93940
www.baypublishing.com

Design by Andrea Gregg
Cover photo by Craig Lovell,
Eagle Visions Photography

Library of Congress
Cataloging-in-Publication
Data available.

CONTRIBUTORS

We would like to thank all of the wineries and businesses that helped make this book come to life.

Baileyana

Buona Tavola Ristorante

Claiborne & Churchill

Eberle Winery

EOS Estate Winery

Hunt Cellars

J. Lohr Vineyards & Wines

Laetitia Vineyard & Winery

Mastantuono Winery

F. McLintocks Restaurant

Opolo Vineyards

Rancho Arroyo Grande Winery & Vineyards

Summerwood Winery & Inn

Vista Del Rey Vineyards

Wild Horse Winery & Vineyards

CONTENTS

WineStyle

PASO ROBLES WINE COUNTRY
SAN LUIS OBISPO WINE COUNTRY

OPOLO VINEYARDS

Some People Collect Stamps...

Opolo Vineyards is the result of a winemaking hobby that "got out of control," according to co-owner Rick Quinn.

What started as a weekend pastime for Rick and his partner Dave Nichols has blossomed into a business that encompasses vineyards spread over 300 acres on both the East and West sides of Paso Robles. The partners are next-door neighbors who happened to share a passion for fine wines and a fascination with the techniques used in growing wine grapes. They set up shop and planted the first Opolo vines in 1996.

From the beginning, the focus was on the fruit, and it has paid off. Some of the most famous names in Napa Valley purchase grapes from Opolo, including St. Supéry, Hess, Neibaum-Coppola and Fetzer as well as Central Coast wineries Wild Horse and Castoro. "We're much bigger farmers than we are winemakers," Rick says.

But that is not to give Opolo wines short shrift. Since the first vintage—a 1999 Cabernet released in 2001 — was made available to the public, Opolo has earned a respectable and growing national recognition. Rick and Dave's wines can be found on the wine lists of such venerable restaurants as Spago, the Ritz-Carlton, the Braemar Country Club in Beverly Hills and the Valley Hunt Club in Pasadena.

Closer to home, the central operation comprises 98 acres of rolling Westside vineyards in as idyllic a setting as the beautiful Paso Robles area offers. The climate here owes a great debt to the nearby Pacific Ocean. The cooling effect of the marine layer accounts for temperature swings — the diurnal range — that can be as great as 50 degrees from afternoon highs to morning lows. This great disparity in temperatures enables the fruit to enjoy a much longer "hang time" and encourages high sugar levels and concentration of flavors.

Opolo also grows wine grapes on 200 acres on the East side of Paso. In contrast, the land is flat and dry and temperatures are much hotter.

Nearly all Opolo wines are estate vintages, meaning that they are vinted from grapes grown by the winery. Curiously, Opolo does not employ a winemaker as such. It's a group effort. Everyone, from owners to "cellar rats" has a say in the wine production. Tasting room manger Genoa Riley believes this approach makes for very consumer-friendly wines that appeal to many people. "There is no dependency on one person's palate although Rick and Dave have the final vote."

The winery has sold out all of the first three years of production, proof of this unique approach.

The people who populate Opolo — the name is from a sassy rosé made on the Dalmatian Coast, a nod to Rick's Serbian heritage — are warm, passionate and down-to-earth. They strive to "take the 'snobbiness' out of wine tasting," Genoa says. They don't want anyone to be intimidated by the process, so the atmosphere at the tasting room is friendly and open.

The room itself is part of the working winery — visitors are surrounded by barrels, and get a real sense of the process of winemaking. A taster will get one-on-one attention here. There are no crowds, so visitors have the opportunity to spend real quality time with one of the owners and learn about Opolo and the wines.

Most weekends, the barbecue is going full-tilt, cranking out Opolo's famous Cevapcici, a special Yugoslav ground meat delicacy or Carne Asada Tacos made from scratch. Hospitality is key here, and everyone thoroughly enjoys a good time.

On a hilltop that commands a striking view of the surrounding hills, a huge

tent is erected each fall for the Harvest Festival. It's a joyous affair. The air is filled with the succulent aroma of whole roasted lamb, taste buds come alive to the nuances of Opolo wines, and the adventurous take off their shoes, roll up their pant legs and have a go at crushing grapes "I Love Lucy" style.

Future plans call for a 12,000-square-foot bed and breakfast and gourmet restaurant to be built on that hilltop. It's a sure bet that when the philosophy that drives Opolo Vineyards is applied to

the hospitality business, the hotel will be booked up months in advance.

No wonder Opolo wines are gaining national recognition. The unique approach taken by Rick and Dave has paid off, and the fruits of their "hobby" are now being savored by thousands of wine lovers all over the United States.

— Michael Chatfield

VISTA DEL REY

"Big Wines from a Small Operation". . .

The term *dry farming* may sound like an oxymoron, but for Dave King, it's a way of life.

On a hilltop six miles north of Paso Robles, 30 miles southeast of Hearst Castle, Dave and his wife and partner Carol have built Vista Del Rey Vineyards. The name translates as "King's View," and a more aptly named piece of land would be hard to come by. Spread before the visitor are miles of rolling hills—many lined with vineyards—that fade into the mist produced by the nearby Pacific Ocean.

The Kings bought this property in 1994. They live and work here, surrounded by the Hacienda Vineyard, planted entirely to Zinfandel. Somehow, the Hacienda Vineyard looks peculiar, until the realization hits that these vines have no trellises, and most mysteriously, no drip irrigation system with black tubes running up and down the rows. The rows of vines look neat, orderly and part of the land, somewhat like an old European vineyard.

The centuries-old technique of dry farming is typically used in areas where rainfall totals less than 20 inches per year. Here—and at the nearby Colina de Robles Vineyard where their acclaimed Barbera is grown—rainfall totals about 13 inches. Although it would be easy to install a drip system and farm grapes like many of his colleagues, Dave prefers this method. He believes that it produces fruit with the more intense, full flavors that define Zinfandel.

This method requires a balance of weather forces that Mother Nature delivers oh-so-rarely. The year 2001 was one such optimum year: rainfall amount, hot, sunny days tempered with cool evenings all came together to create a perfect growing season.

Dave is an outspoken, engaging man, with an impressive depth of knowledge. He has traveled the world courtesy of the U.S. Navy and says that owning and running this vineyard is what he likes to call his "Walter Mitty dream." Vista Del Rey is the embodiment of the American dream of ownership and control of the land and the pioneering spirit and work ethic that first brought settlers to this part of the West.

Dave and Carol operate their modest tasting room as if it were their living room. Guests are made to feel welcome by the family dogs Shylo and Daisy as they lead tasters through their stable of Zinfandel and Barbera vintages. They don't force anything; the taster is allowed to savor and compare. However, suggestions might be made that a nibble of dark chocolate may enhance the experience of this vintage, or that a home-grown walnut may go surprisingly well with another. Unusual for a winery of this size, it's not uncommon for Vista del Rey to have 3-year verticals available for tasting at any given time.

Carol's background is in environmental studies, and she's quick to point out that the operation is a "no kill facility." They don't intentionally take any life here. She has personally relocated snakes, bats and spiders, and minimal pesticides and herbicides are used on the property.

Vista Del Rey is truly a mom-and-pop outfit, in the finest sense of the term. The tasting room is a bit off the beaten path, but a stopover here is well worth the effort.

Daisy

– Michael Chatfield

J. LOHR VINEYARDS & WINES

Focus on Flavor... . . .

Jerry Lohr has a saying he lives by, 'At J. Lohr, we focus on flavor from vine-yard to bottle.' Even before he would succinctly articulate this creed, Jerry was thoroughly evaluating possible vineyard sites that would ultimately reward wine drinkers with wines with the best flavors. With his singular goal to produce wines with genuine depth and flavor, Jerry tasted hundreds of red wines inland and along the coast of California. Impressed by the rich potential of San Luis Obispo County's then little-known Paso Robles, Jerry was one of the early regional winegrowers to stake a claim on property in the Estrella River region and first planted his vineyards in 1986. Today, J. Lohr owns and manages 2,000 acres in the area, and is arguably the largest red wine producer to emerge out of Paso Robles.

A scientist and the son of a South Dakota farming family, Jerry Lohr has combined his two passions in the pursuit of world-class wines. Blending rigorous analytical reasoning with the intuition and hands-on integrity of an artisan farmer, Jerry initially focused his efforts developing the promise of

Monterey County's Arroyo Seco appellation. With its windswept, cool climate and gravelly loam soils, Jerry quickly learned that this region was ideally suited to particular varietals, namely Chardonnay and Riesling, and over the years has grown his vineyards from 280 to 900 acres today. Taking a lesson from the French growing regions of Burgundy and Bordeaux, Jerry understood that great Chardonnay and Cabernet Sauvignon couldn't grow side-by-side. Eager to try new challenges, he began planting Cabernet Sauvignon, Merlot and other red varietals in his new Paso Robles vineyards. Jerry quietly pioneered the Paso Robles appellation, though in recent years his zeal has made him one of the area's most knowledgeable and respected evangelists. For Jerry, getting his hands dirty is an integral part of creating exceptional wine and just plain fun. Unrelenting in his pursuit of the most intense flavors, Jerry is active in every facet of winemaking operations, working alongside his handpicked vineyard team to ensure every viticultural and winemaking step — from cultivating the soil to bottling the wine — culminates in wines with the freshest and most vivid flavors.

The photo of a large, single oak tree atop the highest plateau and overlooking a sweeping grassland hill of vineyards has become emblematic of J. Lohr's presence in Paso Robles and is the home for its Hilltop Cabernet. Critical to flavor development in red varietals are two additional hallmarks of the region, climate and soil. Paso Robles is blessed with consistently hotter days and cooler nights than many other distinguished winegrowing regions. Data from 14,000 weather stations from around the world reveals that Paso Robles has the greatest day and night-time temperature difference of almost any winegrowing region. For Cabernet Sauvignon, a fifty-degree swing in temperature over the course of a twenty-four hour period day is ideal, as hot days allow Cabernet grapes to fully ripen, while cool nights benefit optimum color and tannin development. Harvesting often doesn't begin until the grapes have had a chance to warm up and have reached full flavor. Hand-harvesting of very young and older vines prevents damage, and usually concludes by mid-day when the sun's heat becomes too strong.

This ability to pick grapes at the peak of flavor — coupled with the vineyards' predominantly south-facing slopes and red gravel and limestone soils — produces grapes with intense and concentrated flavors.

Jerry attributes most of J. Lohr's success not only to the careful selection and development of the land but to the company's human capital as well. Dedicated to sustainability not only in farming practices but also in relationships, J. Lohr Vineyards retains a full-time, year-round vineyard crew. The knowledge, energy, and experience J. Lohr's Paso Robles-based employees bring to the vineyards become flavor in the bottle. Turnover is the enemy of consistency and quality, and with very little change in top management in twenty-five years, J. Lohr's group represents one of the most dedicated and experienced teams in the industry.

Jerry's revolutionary stewardship of J. Lohr Vineyards & Wines continues to raise the bar for the entire industry. Constantly experimenting, he and master winemaker Jeff Meier, along with the

efforts of red winemaker Daniel Shaw, are respected for their innovation and exacting standards. Referring to themselves as wine growers, not grape growers, these two leaders have been known to wait almost a decade after acquiring a property to begin planting grapes, as was the case in Monterey's Arroyo Seco appellation. Healthy, balanced soil is a key component to the advancement of flavor in wine. To achieve this, Jerry has created a vineyard development process that minimizes the use of commercial fertilizers by first planting nutrient-rich grain crops that are later harvested back into the soil. Though both labor intensive and expensive, this process fundamentally affects the quality and flavor of every grape.

Another defining J. Lohr process in its commitment to developing wines with the greatest flavors is the use of long-term trials. J. Lohr uses production-size lots for reproducibility, and experiments are often repeated during several consecutive years in order to evaluate results over time. Ongoing areas of experimentation include variations in canopy management, irrigation management and growing vines on soils with high amounts of limestone. But the biggest ongoing experiment at J. Lohr involves evaluating ripeness at harvest to achieve the brightest fruit flavors in all its wine varietals.

Though still run with the loving care of a boutique winery, J. Lohr has wisely invested in state-of-the-art equipment and facilities. One of the few remaining substantial independents, J. Lohr produces only proprietor grown wines. Whether it's the J. Lohr Estates Seven Oaks Cabernet Sauvignon, Estates Los Osos Merlot, Estates South Ridge Syrah or the J. Lohr Hilltop Vineyard Cabernet Sauvignon – among other red wines produced by J. Lohr – each wine is carefully nurtured to realize the full potential of its unique environment. This philosophy has paid off with J. Lohr wines consistently winning high praise and numerous awards for their notable excellence.

An elder statesman of the wine world, Jerry's passion for his work has earned him the respect of his peers and a dedicated following amongst those who appreciate ripe, rich flavors in wines cultivated from one of the nation's most superb appellations — the Paso Robles region of San Luis Obispo County.

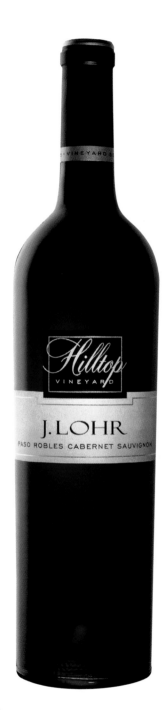

EOS ESTATE WINERY

The Ancient Art of Winemaking . . .

Like their Italian ancestors, brothers Frank and Phil Arciero tend to do things on a grand scale. Having made their fortunes in construction and land development, and dabbled in professional auto racing, the brothers were in search of a new venture. Driving by an expanse of vacant land on Highway 46 in Paso Robles, they were reminded of the fields and farms that surrounded their boyhood village in Italy. Soon after, they began purchasing parcels, about 50 acres at a time. Within a few years, they had accumulated 1,000 acres and in 1983, the first vines were planted.

A few years later it was time to build a winery, and of course, no ordinary winery would do. The 104,000-square-foot winery is an impressive reconstruction of Montecassino, a Benedictine monastery located near Verona. Starting in 1986, wines were produced under the Arciero label in the massive Romanesque structure.

With the arrival of new partners Kerry Vix and the Underwood family during the first half of the '90s, and with the vision of the Arciero family, the winery underwent a spectacular transformation, from its winemaking philosophy to its moniker — EOS Estate Winery. According to Greek mythology, EOS, the Goddess of the Dawn, lifted the sun over the horizon to start each day. The ancient Greeks not only influenced the name, but also when the grapes are harvested — before or right after dawn to keep the fruit cool and help retain the fresh varietal character, and how the wine is crafted—with a focus on artistic quality and traditional winemaking techniques.

Coming to EOS in 1993, senior winemaker Leslie Melendez literally learned the business from the ground up. Shortly after graduating from Cal Poly San Luis Obispo with a degree in nutrition, she joined the winery as a harvest laboratory technician. Immersed in the creative process of winemaking, Leslie immediately knew that she'd discovered her professional calling. "I'm passionate about the craft of winemaking," says Leslie, "and this appellation offers so much in terms of resources, promise and inspiration for my work."

Despite its size and production capacity, the winery continues to craft each award-winning vintage as a varietal that exemplifies the best of the Central Coast appellation.

"We take a minimalist approach to winemaking," Leslie says, "tending rather than processing the wines." And the number of vintages she lovingly 'tends' has grown remarkably during her more-than-a-decade tenure here. With the help of assistant winemaker Chris Rougeot, she is constantly experimenting with everything from barrel selection and toasting to new and ever more challenging production techniques.

Next door to the winery is one of the largest tasting rooms in the Paso Robles AVA. The building showcases their award-winning wines and features a wide range of wine accessories for every season.

There's also a room decorated with photographs and cars from the Arcieros' auto racing days. Leslie is typically on the grounds and will happily share her time with visitors. "I was lucky to have mentors who took time with me to share their understanding and appreciation of wine and the craft of making it," says Leslie. "I want to do the same for today's wine lovers and the winemakers of tomorrow."

– Melanie Bellon Chatfield

WILD HORSE WINERY AND VINEYARDS

Free-spirited Wild Horse Winery is a rare breed. . .

The wild mustangs that once roamed the Carrizo Plains just east of the winery's estate vineyards provide an apt metaphor for the winemaking team at Wild Horse. Free-spirited and driven by an unbridled passion for quality, Wild Horse Winery is a rare breed.

Founded by Central Coast wine pioneer Ken Volk, and now led by winemaker, Mark Cummins, Wild Horse has been devoted to creating fine wines that reflect the distinctive character, diversity and beauty of this region for more than two decades. Gently swirling a glass of any of their superb vintages under the nose or indulging in a sip confirms their success.

Creativity is not only appreciated here, it's encouraged and fostered. While these maverick winemakers are serious about their craft, there's a contagious playfulness and genuine friendliness that make one want to return. They consider it their mission to craft wines that enhance the enjoyment of life for

wine lovers from the novice to the expert. This friendly, accessible approach to wine is evident in Wild Horse's tasting room, cellar and in each vintage.

The 46-acre vineyard in Templeton is as much a viticultural science lab as it is home to the Wild Horse estate vineyards. The breakthrough processes — some patented — encompass everything from trellising, crop protection, irrigation and water reclamation systems to vineyard management and the winemaking itself. In the 1990s, Wild Horse adopted a brilliant, earth-friendly

approach to pest control. Using a remote controlled model airplane, they disperse "good" insects over the vineyards to feed on the "bad" ones. The paratrooper pests have proven to be an effective defense against insect related crop damage.

Sustainable farming and environmental sensitivity are a way of life here. "When you're a good steward of the land and focus on working with what nature gives you, nature gives back," says Scott Welcher, Viticulturist and General Manager at Wild Horse. "We want you to taste the vineyard."

The acreage is divided into small growing lots, each with characteristics and microclimates suited to one of more than a dozen varietals, including rare and little known varieties such as Vermentino, Verdelho and Blaufrankisch. About ten percent of the grapes for the winery's overall production are grown on the estate, while the remainder is sourced from more than 40 vineyards within the Central Coast appellation.

Fruit harvested from each area of the estate and other vineyards is picked, vinified and kept separate until blending. And at Wild Horse, blending is an art form. "We've come to expect certain characteristics in the grapes from each area and blend the best of those to achieve a particular style for each vintage," explains Cummins.

Wild Horse Winery and Vineyards produces an impressive range of varietals including what they like to call their "four horsemen" — Merlot, Pinot Noir, Chardonnay and Cabernet Sauvignon. A second label — Cheval Sauvage, French for Wild Horse, is reserved for exceptional bottlings of their flagship varietal, Pinot Noir. Whether white or red, spicy or subtle, for savoring alone or enjoying with food, you'll taste the free-spirited creativity and a respect for tradition in every vintage.

— Melanie Bellon Chatfield

BUONA TAVOLA RISTORANTE

Where the Secret Ingredient is Love...

Carpaccio del Monte Bianco, risotto ai porcini e erbe silvane, nodino di manzo ai sapori delle alpi, insalata del Dante, tiramisu, vino rosso. Admittedly it reads like a dinner order in Tuscany, yet fortunately it's much closer to home — at Buona Tavola (good table) in Paso Robles and San Luis Obispo. The food, the wine, the attentive, personal service, the sophisticated décor and Italian chef and owner Antonio Varia all contribute to the enticing atmosphere of this elegant yet casual trattoria.

Given the superb quality of the cuisine, Buona Tavola might be more aptly named Magnifico Tavola. Antonio fuses the best of the region's fresh herbs and vegetables, seafood and meats with porcini mushrooms, polenta, prosciutto, olive oil and other treasures from Italy into what he calls "a lighter approach to Northern Italian cuisine."

Describing the wine-friendly food here often requires words typically reserved for fine vintages — aromatic, earthy, elegantly balanced and superbly textured with a lingering finish.

"The first thing I tell my chefs and everyone in the kitchen is that each dish should be made like you are making it for your family or yourself," says Antonio in his captivatingly melodic Italian accent. And family is just what you feel like at Buona Tavola. The wait staff is professional, welcoming and they know a thing or two about wine. As a team, they've tasted both the food and wine so there's always someone who can give you a first-hand recommendation.

Wine is an integral part of the meal at most Italian dining tables and Buona Tavola is no exception. It's exceptional, and they have the awards to prove it. Buona Tavola received the Wine Spectator "Award of Excellence" in 2002, 2003, & 2004.

In addition to Buona Tavola's award-winning wine list, the Paso Robles restaurant has a full bar offering Italian spirits such as Grappa, Frernet Branca, Vin Santo and Amaro along with exquisite classic Martinis, a nice collection of Ports and all the cocktail standards.

Born in the charming town of Armeno in Northern Italy's Piemonte region, Antonio inherited a love of cooking from his father, also an accomplished chef. After completing his studies at the

Scuola Maggia di Stresa, he apprenticed at restaurants throughout Northern Italy. He furthered his training in some of Europe's finest hotels and on the Princess Cruise Lines. He came ashore in Los Angeles in the 1980s and served as Executive Chef in several of that city's finest restaurants. Venturing out on his own in 1992, he opened Buona Tavola in downtown San Luis Obispo. Its overwhelming success and a growing demand inspired Antonio's second Buona Tavola in the heart of Paso Robles' wine country in 2001.

When you dine at either location or attend one of the many wine dinners and special

events that Antonio caters, you'll discover the secret ingredient that makes Buona Tavola's cuisine memorable: love. Antonio says: "I cook with love."

—Melanie Bellon Chatfield

41

SUMMERWOOD WINERY AND INN

Relax with a glass of wine — at Summerwood . . .

Idyllic. No other word more aptly describes Summerwood Winery and Inn. The charming white inn, surrounded by fragrant herb and flower gardens and productive vineyards, is Paso Robles' only four diamond rated inn. The equally charming tasting room and winery are just a few steps across a quiet country road. The sunlight-splashed tasting room has the feel of an elegant lodge with its stately fireplace, comfortable seating areas, handsome wood and brass bar and adjoining outdoor brick patio. One wall of the tasting area is glass and overlooks the wine production area itself, enabling visitors to watch winemaker Scott Hawley at work while sampling the fruits of his labors.

A stay at Summerwood leaves one refreshed in the truest sense of the word. Each of the Bed and Breakfast's nine rooms, one a suite perched privately above the others, is adorned uniquely in an American Country style and offers a lovely view. While the esthetics and wine are enough to lure repeat visitors, the amenities and gourmet cuisine make it a certainty.

There's an attention to detail that leaves little to chance, yet the ambience is utterly free of hustle and bustle. The experience is beautifully orchestrated to induce a state of comfort and tranquility — from the initial welcome right through to the staff waving as one reluctantly drives away. Every afternoon in

the expansive yet cozy great room, guests are treated to Summerwood wines and gourmet appetizers prepared by Executive Chef Charlie Paladin Wayne. He masterfully conducts food preparation for inn guests as well as

quick-to-sell-out wine dinners and special events. Upon returning from dinner, the aromas of freshly brewed coffee and warm-from-the-oven cookies await. A bottle of wine, turn-down service with yet another special treat, plush robes and spa amenities help make each room a haven of leisure and retreat. A cooked to order gourmet breakfast featuring seasonal delicacies is a wonderful way to start the day.

Back in the tasting room, the friendly, knowledgeable staff is more than happy to share their love of Summerwood's fine vintages with visitors. A sense of being rushed is completely absent here. Since the inaugural release of their 2001 vintages in 2003, Summerwood has enjoyed a steady increase in loyal patrons. Their wines are on the lists of a few fine local restaurants,

but are otherwise available only through the tasting room and their Seasons Club. All of their wines are exceptional, and the 2001 Diosa — a blend of Rhône varietals Syrah, Mourvédre and Grenache aged in a combination of French and American Oak barrels — is the type of wine for which wine-words were created.

Syrah and Cabernet Sauvignon grapes occupy 36 of the more than 40 acres of Summerwood's estate vineyards on the western and more ocean-influenced side of Paso Robles. Grapes are sourced from other Paso Robles and Central Coast vineyards to complete their 5,500 annual case production. Current plans are to reach a maximum production of 10,000 cases within six years. "That will be our ceiling," says Scott. "We want to keep the quantity down so that we can keep the quality up. Our whole operation is designed to make great wines."

According to Hawley, great wines start in the vineyard. "Sourcing is

important to me," explains Scott. "We work closely with each vineyard manager and concentrate on those in western Paso Robles for our red wine program and other areas of the Central Coast region for our whites."

Scott likes to think of his wines as the offspring of Mother Nature and modern technology. "Each vintage is representative of its environment. We use technology to help us more accurately interrupt nature's instructions. And I only get one shot a year to do this right."

Fortunately for the connoisseur of fine wine and the lover of superb accommodations, Summerwood is a relatively young winery and inn. The award-winning vintages that have already made their debut offer promise of even greater things to come. And memories of a sojourn at the inn will loudly beckon the visitor to a speedy return.

— Melanie Bellon Chatfield

EBERLE WINERY

The University of Paso Robles . . .

No one would accuse Gary Eberle of small thinking.

Quite the contrary. He dreams big. He builds big. And he lives big.

Eberle Winery is a testament to Gary's thinking. When his winery outgrew its original 10,000 case-per-year capacity, he went underground — literally. Utilizing huge machines normally used for Welsh mining equipment, he tunneled 16,000 square feet of caves in the hill under the tasting room and its parking lot. In the caves, the barrels are filled and emptied using gravity alone, a practice that dovetails with the overall Eberle philosophy of "kind and gentle" wine treatment. Gary says that cave aging is "the ultimate way to treat wine kindly."

Lining the walls for what seems like miles are French and American oak barrels stacked three high. A unique system utilizes specially-designed stainless steel bars that keep the barrels accessible and stable. So stable, in fact, that not a drop of wine was lost in the December 2003 earthquake.

The Eberle story began in the late 1960s, when Gary arrived in California in a six-year-old Pontiac towing a U-Haul full of hand-me-down furniture. He had $800 in his pocket, and a desire to make fine wine. With a degree in biology, Gary was doing graduate work in New Orleans when a professor introduced him to the world of fine food and wine. It was a fascination with Cabernet Sauvignon that led him to the idea of creating American wines that would rival those of Bordeaux.

Four decades later, Eberle wins "more than our fair share of medals," according to Gary. The operation produces more than 25,000 cases of premium wines per year — a large production facility that maintains the quality control of a small boutique winery. Surprisingly, fully half of that production is sold from the tasting room at the winery on Highway 46 East, six miles east of Paso Robles. Gary maintains that this is the most successful tasting room south of the Napa Valley in terms of cases sold and dollar volume. It's a beautiful room, with an expansive wooden bar, vast selection of wine-related merchandise, and an inviting picnic area overlooking the vineyards. Most importantly, it's staffed with an extremely knowledgeable and enthusiastic team of professionals.

A particular point of pride for Gary is the number of talented professionals who have worked for him and gone on to greatness on their own. He is fond of calling his winery "The University of Paso Robles."

Early on in his education, one of his professors gave Gary a piece of advice that he lives by to this day: "What's in the bottle should taste like what's on the vine." As a grower, he strives to produce the best fruit possible. As a winemaker, he believes his job is "not to screw it up."

After spending some time at the Eberle tasting room tasting the wines produced here, it becomes apparent that no one around here is screwing anything up; quite the opposite.

Many think that Gary gets it just right.

— Michael Chatfield

MASTANTUONO WINERY

A spirited, expressive, old-world style that's tutto l'italiano

"The conditions were perfect for our first three vintages — 1977, 1978 and 1979—and the wines were outstanding," says Pasquale Mastantuono, founder and head winemaker at Mastantuono Winery in Templeton. "We've spent every year since trying to top ourselves."

Wearing tall rubber boots folded down to fit his small frame, eight-year-old Pasquale climbed atop his grandfather's wine press, beginning his initiation into the world of winemaking. When he was thirteen, his father sold a thriving grocery business in Detroit, bought a new 1951 Buick and moved the family to Central California. While it wasn't difficult to envision himself as a winemaker, Pasquale decided to follow in his father's footsteps — building a successful retail business. He sold it in the mid-'70s to pursue his dream of winemaking full time, becoming one of the first vintners to see the potential of Paso Robles as a premier wine region.

Today, Mastantuono Winery produces up to 10,000 cases a year, including his flagship Zinfandel. Also featured are prized Italian varietals such as Barbera, Sangiovese and Muscat Canelli and wine-world staples, Cabernet Sauvignon, Merlot, Chardonnay and others. The staggering array, crafted from grapes grown on his acreage and in other vineyards under his supervision, also features a California Port and Champagne. "It's actually sparkling wine but I call it 'Champagne' to irritate the French!" This playful antagonism is a trait that served Pasquale well in blazing the trail for the county's booming wine industry.

According to Pasquale, the road to a great vintage is best traveled by "steering" the wine in the right direction. "If the grapes don't have it from a viticulture perspective, they won't make a great wine," Pasquale says. "We start with exceptional grapes and guide the process to achieve the drinkable, full-of-fruit, food-friendly qualities our wines are known for."

Among local restaurateurs, Mastantuono is also known for innovation. A few years back, while dining with his wife at a local Mexican restaurant, Pasquale discovered an unmet need. With a license for beer and wine only, the establishment had come up against a seemingly unbeatable foe — creating an authentic tasting margarita with wine. "They were using a prepared margarita mix and White Zinfandel," recalls Pasquale. "And it wasn't pretty."

Up for a challenge, he went back to his lab and two years later presented his creation — San Luis Tequila Wine. "It's made with agave and grapes and it's 40 proof," he says. "The rest is a secret." Many a wine taster has been surprised by the aroma of Tequila in the tasting room. And even more so by the authenticity the Tequila Wine adds to a wine-made margarita.

Although born in the U.S. to Italian emigrant parents, Pasquale Mastantuono's style is tutto l'italiano. From an obvious love of family, friends and food to music and a rousing game of bocce ball, time with Pasquale is like a trip to old Napoli. There's a spirited, expressive, old-world style unmistakably evident in his character, and in his award-winning wines.

— Melanie Bellon Chatfield

HUNT CELLARS

A Symphony of Wines . . .

. . ."The finish is the hardest part of winemaking," says David Hunt. He views a good finish as an invitation that lures the wine lover to the next sip, and to the next bottle. In his relentless pursuit of excellence, he labors over the wine, constantly urging it toward the perfect balance that he aspires to. "I literally lose sleep over my wine; it's like having children." He hovers over his creations at every step in the process, and it's not unusual to see him making changes up to the very day the wine is bottled.

This attention to detail has not been lost on wine experts. Every wine in the Hunt Cellars lineup has won Best of Class, a Gold Medal or has scored in the 90's in competitions across the country. David is a highly competent, competitive and driven individual, as is evident in even a short conversation.

Some would describe him as a renaissance man: successful professional musician, technology pioneer, real estate developer and now highly accomplished and respected winemaker. What makes these accomplishments even more impressive is the fact that David Hunt is blind. He doesn't dwell on it. Far from it. In fact, he credits his loss of sight with sharpening his other senses, most notably his acute senses of smell and taste. "There are only two blind professional winemakers in history — Dom Perignon and me," he states.

When he decided to turn his lifelong love of food and wine into a profession, David launched a state-wide search for the perfect conditions in which to grow the fine grapes necessary to produce the wines he envisioned. He was introduced to the west side of Paso Robles in 1996. The combination of soil diversity and an

optimum growing climate in the region convinced him that he had found his land. Purchasing 550 acres of hilltop and mountainous acres, he established Destiny Vineyards, named after his daughter. Today, Hunt Cellars produces over 8,000 cases per year, with 90% coming from Destiny Vineyards which enjoys 50 degree swings in weather during the growing season, creating concentrated intense varietal character.

David's professional music career included well-known artists such as Ambrosia and David Benoit. His love of music is reflected in the names he has bestowed upon his wines: "Rhapsody in Red" a Super Tuscan, "Harmony" Merlot, "Serenade" Syrah, "Moonlight Sonata" Chardonnay, "Starlight Concerto" Sauvignon Blanc and "Good Vibrations" Port.

That playful spirit carries over into the tasting room, a bright, sunny, inviting building on Highway 46, three miles west of Highway 101. One area is dominated by a white baby grand piano where David will occasionally hold forth for family, friends and lucky visitors. The staff here is warm, friendly and very knowledgeable. They guide the taster through the entire range of Hunt Cellars offerings, making informed food pairing recommendations and helping novices with the finer points of wine tasting.

In the case of Hunt Cellars, the man and his wines are very much alike: assertive without being overbearing, bold but not obnoxious, and committed to attaining a balance that translates to a smooth, memorable finish.

– Michael Chatfield

PASO ROBLES

Paso Robles: the jewel of the Central Coast

Little Paso Robles is growing up.

The growth in this central coast hamlet can only be described as explosive. Just a few years ago, the town of El Paso de Robles—Paso Robles to you and me, "Paso" to locals—was known to many Californians as a place to stop for gas between Los Angeles and San Francisco, and where you could catch the connector road to Interstate 5. Others knew it for the astonishing number of big-name entertainers that regularly headline at the annual California Mid-State Fair.

But today, more and more wine and food aficionados are beating a path to Paso Robles. Why? Well, for one thing, the number of premium wineries and acreage devoted to growing wine grapes more than doubled between 1993 and 2002. Within a stone's throw of the idyllic town square of Paso, there are now around 80 bonded wineries producing more than 26 million cases of wine each year. Many, if not most,

of those wineries operate tasting rooms that are now attracting visitors from all over the world to the next great area of California winemaking.

There was a time, not that long ago, when fine cuisine here meant a Papa burger at the local A&W drive-in, washed down with some of that superb root beer or maybe a couple of adult beers. Today, there are numerous

restaurants that will please the palate of even the most discriminating gourmet — and more are on the way.

Some compare the Paso Robles AVA to what Napa Valley was like in the 1980s — a place just beginning to boom, a town still small enough to have neighbors who go next door to borrow a cup of sugar, or a bottle of wine. It is

also a region where vintners and winemakers are just beginning to tap the full potential of the climate and growing conditions.

West of town, the topography is comprised of slightly-more-than-gently rolling hills, part of the Santa Lucia Mountains that define the Salinas Valley of Monterey County to the north. The soil is rocky, providing the excellent drainage that allows vintners to achieve the precise balance of water and nutrients that allows the grapes to develop rich, complex flavors.

On the other side of the Salinas River, the land flattens out and takes on a valley-floor-like appearance. To the east the soils are made up of sediments formed during the Pleistocene Age and carried here by the river. Being more compacted, root growth is limited. The ocean influence is not as strong here, but is still felt. While the fog does not penetrate here as strongly as to the west, the temperatures are still mitigated by the cool breezes generated by the sea.

In the words of one grower, "Paso Robles is the only place left in California where an aspiring wine maker can get started." Wine lovers everywhere can rejoice in that fact. It means that many, many more superb wines will be produced in Paso Robles.

— Michael Chatfield

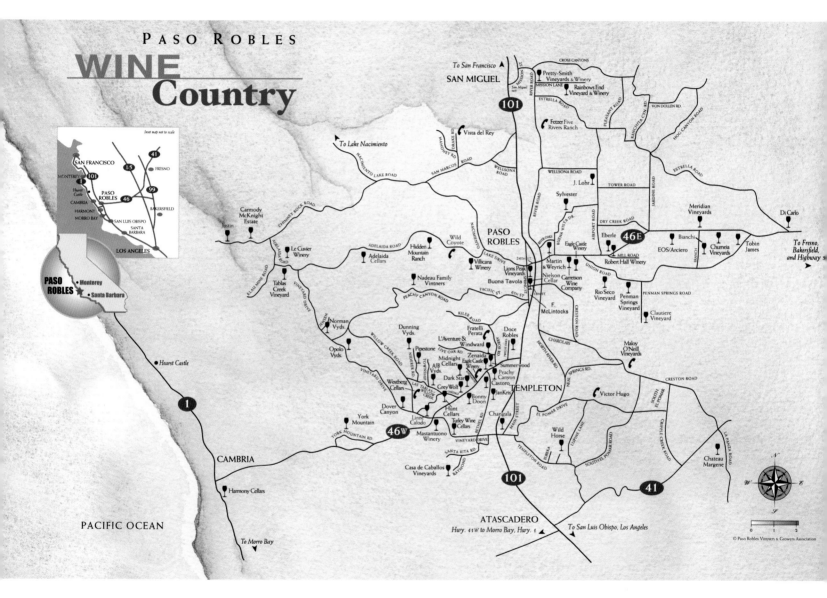

PASO ROBLES
WINE
Country

San Miguel
To San Francisco

Pretty-Smith Vineyards & Winery
Cross Canyons
Rainbows End Vineyard & Winery
Mission Lane
Estrella Road
Fetzer Five Rivers Ranch
Pleasant Road
Von Dollen Rd.
Hog Canyon Road

To Lake Nacimiento
Vista del Rey
Mahovey Rd.
Drake Rd.
San Marcos Road
Wellsona Road

Wellsona Road
J. Lohr
Tower Road
Jardine Road
Estrella Road

Sylvester
Meridian Vineyards
Di Carlo

Carmody McKnight Estate
Justin
Chimney Rock Road
Adelaida Road
Wild Coyote
Hidden Mountain Ranch
PASO ROBLES
Lake Drive
24th St.
Eberle
46E
Bianchi
EOS/Arciero
Chumeia Vineyards
Tobin James
To Fresno, Bakersfield, and Highway 5

Le Cuvier Winery
Adelaida Cellars
Villicana Winery
Lions Peak Vineyards
Martin & Weyrich
Eagle Castle Winery
Robert Hall Winery

Tablas Creek Vineyard
Nadeau Family Vintners
Buona Tavola
Nielson Cellar
Carretson Wine Company
Rio Seco Vineyard
Penman Springs Road
Penman Springs Vineyard
Clautiere Vineyard

Peachy Canyon Road
Pacific St.
6th St.
F. McLintocks

Norman Vyds.
Kiler Road
Charolais

Dunning Vyds.
Fratelli Perata
Doce Robles
Maloy O'Neill Vineyards

Opolo Vyds.
Pipestone
L'Aventure & Windward
Live Oak Rd.
Midnight Cellars
Zenaida
Summerwood
AJB Vyds.
Eagle Castle Winery
Peachy Canyon
Castoro
TEMPLETON
Victor Hugo

Dark Star
Grey Wolf
JanKris
North River Rd.
Neal Springs Rd.
Creston Road

Westberg Cellars
Bonny Doon

Dover Canyon
Hunt Cellars
Changala
El Pomar Drive

Linne Calodo
Turley Wine Cellars
46W
York Mountain
Mastantuono Winery
Wild Horse
Chateau Margene

York Mountain Rd.
Vineyard Drive
Ethel Rd.
Templeton Road
La Panza Rd.

Santa Rita Rd.
Casa de Caballos Vineyards
101

CAMBRIA

Hearst Castle

Harmony Cellars

ATASCADERO
Hwy. 41W to Morro Bay, Hwy. 1
To San Luis Obispo, Los Angeles

PACIFIC OCEAN

To Morro Bay

Inset map
San Francisco
Monterey
101
41
Fresno
I-5
Paso Robles
Cambria
46
Harmony
Morro Bay
San Luis Obispo
99
Bakersfield
Santa Barbara
Los Angeles
Inset map not to scale

PASO ROBLES
Monterey
Santa Barbara

© Paso Robles Vintners & Growers Association

MAP COURTESY OF PASO ROBLES VINTNERS AND GROWERS ASSOCIATION • WWW.PASOWINE.COM • 2003

SAN LUIS OBISPO WINE COUNTRY

A Mecca for Wine Lovers . . .

From the beautiful beaches of Pismo to the shopping of Atascadero; from the wilderness areas of the Los Padres National Forest to the grandeur of William Randolph Hearst's San Simeon; from the rich historical heritage of the California Missions to the cutting edge research at California Polytechnic State University, the diversity of land, nature and humanity have made San Luis Obispo County a hotbed of economic and social growth.

In 2004, the San Luis (pronounced LOO-is, not LOO-ee) Obispo area — encompassing Atascadero and Paso Robles — was rated the third best place to live in the United States by Cities Ranked and Rated, an annual book that ranks cities using a set of criteria across nine categories including economy, climate, education, and arts and culture.

And now this area, located halfway between Los Angeles and San Francisco, has become a Mecca for wine lovers, attracted by still-growing number of winemakers and their tasting rooms that have become established in the area.

South San Luis Obispo County is the site of two American Viticultural Areas (AVAs): the Edna Valley and the Arroyo Grande Valley. These areas, along with the Avila Valley and Nipomo, have been the scene of a tremendous growth in the wine industry, especially in the last decade of the twentieth century.

Wine grape cultivation in the region dates back at least 200 years, when Franciscan padres under the direction of Father Junipero Serra planted grapes at the Mission San Miguel Archangel, in present day downtown San Luis Obispo. No one knows just what varietals they planted, but we do know that the wines they produced earned the padres higher revenues than any other wine-producing mission in California.

That set the stage for the premium and ultra-premium wines produced today in the county.

Jack and Catharine Niven are regarded as catalysts for the burgeoning wine industry of today. After selling their family interest in a San Francisco Bay Area grocery chain, they pursued their dream of growing premium wine grapes and chose land in the Edna Valley, southeast of the city of San Luis Obispo. They founded Paragon Vineyards and between 1973 and 1975 planted 550 acres, finding over time that the terroir of the region was ideally suited to Chardonnay and Pinot Noir. Today, Pinot Noir is considered the flagship grape of the region, with local wineries producing Pinots that win awards around the world. In recent years, many producers have also discovered the region to be particularly well-suited to Rhone varietals such as Syrah.

A wine tasting tour of San Luis Obispo County is a delightful way to spend an afternoon, a weekend — or a week. The area has a range of charming accommodations and restaurants that would be at home in San Francisco or L.A. Most wineries, large and small, operate tasting rooms staffed by enthusiastic wine lovers who live to share their knowledge with visitors.

The San Luis Obispo Vintners and Growers Association maintains a helpful Web site that contains maps, winery/vineyard information, a calendar of intriguing wine events and more. Before you visit SLO, make sure to visit www.slowine.com.

— Michael Chatfield

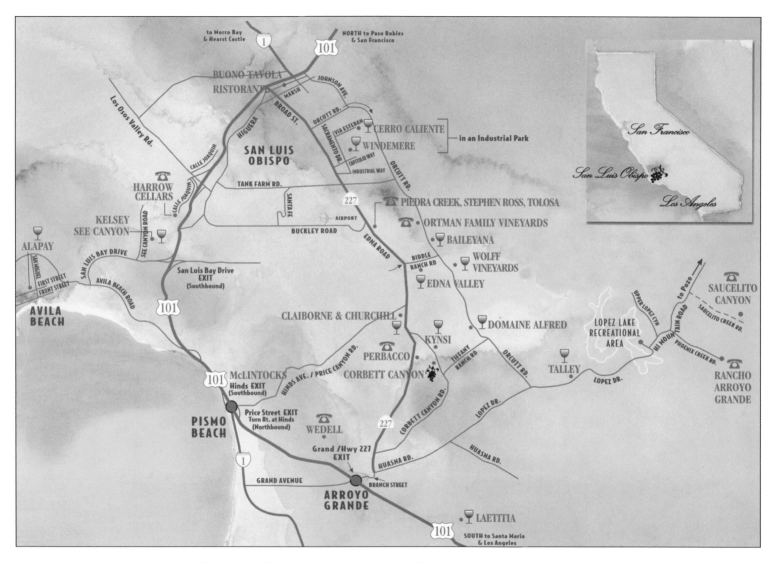

Map courtesy of San Luis Obispo Vintners and Growers Association • www.slowine.com

RANCHO ARROYO GRANDE WINERY & VINEYARDS

Bottling the Spirit of the Old West

Driving the perimeter of the sprawling, 4,000-acre Rancho Arroyo Grande, one notices a unique feature — fences made of rocks that bear the delicate imprints of fossilized oyster shells. Not something you'd expect to see on a working ranch located 12 miles inland. Steeped in California's early history, the ranch was originally a Spanish land grant, serving as a support station for Mission San Luis Obispo and as a stopover for road-weary travelers. Later in the 19th Century, vineyards of the St. Remy Winery graced portions of the land. Today, the ranch is once again home to vineyards and two distinct wineries — Rancho Arroyo Grande Winery and Vineyard and River Wild Winery.

In 1997 Gary and Thereza Verboon, entrepreneurs from Southern California purchased Rancho Arroyo Grande. They had a strong suspicion the unique conditions of soil, climate and elevation could combine to become the perfect combination for the production of world class Zinfandel and Rhone style wines. They asked full-time ranch manager Todd Ruffoni if he wouldn't mind

watching the vines and Todd was happy to apply his extensive land-management skills to a new type of crop. Gary's new love of winegrowing quickly blossomed into a full-fledge passion. Today, more than 265 acres of vineyards now share the land with 6,000 olive trees, 300 head of beef cattle, 35 quarter horses and abundant wild life. An expansive, yet eco-friendly and energy efficient winery, tasting room and education complex is under construction on the ranch, slated for a 2006 opening.

An "extended winemaking family" that includes some of the most highly-respected vintners in the Central Coast region crafts wines under the two labels. The vineyards that produce the Rancho Arroyo Grande premium estate wines were planted in 1998 on the hillsides, sloping plains and remote plateaus of the vast ranch. The 80-acre Potrero Vineyard, perched at 800-feet, is

dry-farmed and planted primarily with Zinfandel, with some Syrah, Sauvignon Blanc and Viognier. Dry farming creates a special challenge for the vines, yielding intensely flavored and beautifully colored grapes. Rancho Arroyo Grande's inaugural release was a limited 2001 vintage.

The River Wild Winery is the second label, the one under which the Mossy Oak Wild Game Blends are bottled. In a move unusual for the wine industry, Gary Verboon and Bob Steddum, marketing manager, teamed up with Mossy Oak, the nation's leader in outdoor camouflage in 2003 to launch a one-of-a-kind wine brand. It was an ingenious move, really, creating a line of wines that pair perfectly with wild game, fish and fowl. The wines also happen to pair beautifully with store-bought

meats, fish and poultry and vegetarian dishes. Marketed nationwide through sporting associations, conservation groups and hunting clubs, these wines are loaded for bear. "Our goal is the elimination of intimidation," quips Bob in regard to removing the mystique of wine drinking for the sportsman. And in the true spirit of the sportsman, the winery gives back to the environment that gives so freely to the hunter. A portion of proceeds from the sale of the Wild Game Blend wines supports conservation organizations including the National Wild Turkey Foundation and Safari Club International.

The label for each of the four wines — Trout Blend, Waterfowl Blend, Venison Blend, and Turkey Blend — is bordered by the type of camoflague worn by the hunter of that particular game. And while it may at first sound like a matter of clever packaging, these are serious wines carefully researched and

blended to pair with specific types of foods. Like their Rancho Arroyo Grande counterparts, the Mossy Oak Wild Game Blends are first-class vintages. Their creation was guided by the expertise of renowned winemaker Eric Hickey who served as a consultant to develop the blends.

Winemaker Clarissa Nagy, formerly director of winery research at another California winery, is fairly new to the operation and her experience promises great things for the future of these two labels.

The half-rugged, half-tamed terrain of Rancho Arroyo Grande embodies the spirit of the pioneer — a feisty

courage to explore, test and discover, ever mindful of the ultimate rule of mother nature. It's in that spirit that Gary and Thereza Verboon and their band of ranching and wine-making pioneers set out to revisit the ranch's past as a wine producing land. In bottling the spirit of the Old West, they've managed to bring home a trophy in the vintages of Rancho Arroyo Grande and River Wild.

— Melanie Bellon Chatfield

CLAIBORNE & CHURCHILL

An Education in Winemaking . . .

There is an ancient Norse proverb: "Wine should be drunk with a friend."
One doesn't generally think of ancient Vikings as connoisseurs of fine wine,
but Clay Thompson inscribed the label of his 2001 Runestone Pinot Noir with
that bit of wisdom.

Clay and his wife and partner Fredericka Churchill took a huge leap of faith to
found Claiborne and Churchill in the early 1980s. Both were teachers at the
University of Michigan—he of Old Norse languages and literature, she of
German. During a lecture trip to UCLA and UC Berkeley in the spring of
1981, they toured the nascent wine regions of California. While visiting Edna
Valley Winery, Clay was bitten by the wine bug and impulsively asked how one
got started in the wine business.

The following August he found himself working for six dollars an hour as a "cellar rat" at Edna Valley. Fredericka and Clay had married, and to keep the wolves from their door while her husband learned winemaking from the bottom up, she worked in a bookstore, and then taught at Cal Poly in San Luis Obispo. Later, she became a salesperson, learning the business end of the industry.

Their radical transformation from the halls of academia to the vineyards and wineries of Central California was complete with the founding of Claiborne & Churchill in 1983. At first, they rented space in a warehouse in San Luis Obispo. There, they began making wines that stress Germanic fruit flavors while keeping sugars to a minimum, much like the wines produced in the French/German border region of Alsace, an area they both love. "We do march to our own drummer as far as wine production is concerned," Clay says.

American wine fanciers typically regard Riesling and Gewurztraminer as sweet wines when in fact, they can be crisp and lively, and are some of the world's best food wines. Even putting the word "**dry**" in front of the varietal name doesn't always catch people's attention. So Clay and Fredericka have had to rely on the skills honed during their first careers and become educators again.

Once initiated, people become true believers. The C&C Cellar Club has nearly a thousand members — this for a winery that produces only 6,000-7,000 case per year. And the wines have earned many awards and accolades at competitions not only in the U.S., but, amazingly for an American producer, in Alsace itself at the International Riesling Competition.

Claiborne & Churchill has come a long way since their days in that out-of-the-way warehouse in San Luis Obispo. The year 1995 saw the completion of a production facility on Carpenter Canyon Road, in a bucolic rural setting amid rolling hills and green pastures. A straw bale building — the first of its kind in California — also houses a charming and comfortable tasting room, where tasters learn that not all Germanic wines are sweet, that it is possible to successfully change careers in mid-life, and that, indeed, wine is best enjoyed with friends.

—Michael Chatfield

LAETITIA VINEYARD AND WINERY

Joy and Happiness from the Arroyo Grande Valley . . .

Lucky the llama doesn't understand Latin. He doesn't have to, because he already knows that Laetitia means joy, happiness and delight. The llama meanders in his pasture overlooking the 1,800-acre estate. Lucky lives a life envied by many: he gets to spend all his time in a vineyard.

And it's a beautiful vineyard. Situated in the Arroyo Grande Valley, it affords heavenly views of surrounding orchards and the nearby Pacific Ocean. The property is above the fog line, but the marine influence is still felt as summer's daytime heat is moderated by cool evening sea breezes.

The vineyard was originally planted by Champagne Deutz for their American venture, Maison Deutz. The land was chosen because of its similarity to that of Epérnay, France. This is one of California's coolest grape-growing regions, eminently suitable for Chardonnay and especially Pinot Noir. In 1997 the operation was renamed Laetitia and the focus was shifted to still wines in the Burgundian style.

Dave Hickey is Laetitia's sparkling winemaker. For him, fine sparkling wine is the result of superior grapes. "The progress we have made in our estate vineyards has had a tremendous impact on the quality of our sparkling wines," he says.

Laetitia is a family affair: the winery is owned by successful businessman Selim Zilkha and his daughter Nadia Wellisz, who oversees marketing. Eric Hickey, Dave's son, is head winemaker and General Manager of the operation. He apprenticed at the winery beginning when he was just 16. Eric is trained in the French style and underwent some training in France.

The still wines of Laetitia are produced in three tiers: Estate Wines are Pinot Noir, Chardonnay, Pinot Blanc and Syrah. Reserve Wines are crafted from the finest fruit, selected by Eric and are strictly limited in production. Single Vineyard Pinot Noirs are the crème de la crème, made only in years of exceptional fruit quality.

Of course, Laetitia also produces premium sparkling wines. Dave crushes these grapes in two Ateliers Coquard basket presses (the only ones of their kind in the U.S.). This old-world method contrasts sharply with the technology used to "riddle" the wine. Typically, Champagne bottles are stored at a slight downward angle in racks during fermentation and rotated — riddled — at prescribed intervals to allow sediment to collect in the neck for later removal. Except for a few select vintages, Laetitia sparkling wines are riddled in a huge, computer-controlled device that looks like a cross between a Calder sculpture and a midway carnival ride.

The general public probably won't get to see this machine in action, but they can visit the pristine tasting room, sited on a hill that showcases that lovely view. The original winery, including the basket presses, is adjacent to the room, and there are lovely picnic grounds and a demonstration vineyard.

For Lucky, all this is secondary. He is more interested in what's in the next pasture than in what people do with all those grapes. Count us lucky that the people who run Laetitia know exactly what to do with them: produce exceptional wines of outstanding quality.

— Michael Chatfield

F. McLINTOCKS

Beef

"Beef. It's what's for dinner... and for lunch the next day!" . . .

A steak house in a book called *WineStyle*? F. McLintocks is here for good reason. Red wine with red meat is a culinary match made in carnivore heaven. Located in the heart of the Central Coast wine region, the family-owned restaurant features some of the area's most acclaimed wine producers, where McLintocks serves only 100 percent USDA Choice corn-fed beef.

It's impossible to visit F. McLintocks Saloon and Dining House and not have a good time. If the rustic décor — liberally sprinkled with antique ranching implements and including ranch brands designed by customers — doesn't get you to crack a smile, then certainly the antics of the serving staff will. Your bus person will perform amazing feats of derring-do involving ice water, a glass on your head and a blindfold. And if it's your birthday, you're in for a real treat: you'll be serenaded and presented with a decadent strawberry shortcake with a candle and a cherry on top.

It's also impossible to leave McLintocks hungry. Every dinner includes onion rings, salsa, a choice of salads, Trail Camp beans, garlic bread and Ranch Fried potatoes. Beans, bread and potatoes are refilled at your pleasure. And after all that, you are treated to a liqueur or a serving of sherbet or ice cream. Bear in mind: this is in *addition* to an absolutely huge array of entrée choices.

The focus here is on meat, and plenty of it. From a petite 10-ounce Top Sirloin or Filet Mignon to a huge 24-ounce T-Bone or Porterhouse, any steak on our menu can be extra-cut for a charge. Expert butchers age and trim all the meat on-site in a spotless butcher shop at the flagship Shell Beach location.

And McLintocks doesn't skimp on the beverages either. Order a martini or other specialty drink and you will be presented with a 16-ounce Mason jar and your own cocktail strainer. The wine list leans toward the reds, as one might imagine, but many whites of outstanding quality are offered. The wines of the Central Coast region are well represented, featuring those of EOS, Wild Horse and Baileyana.

Founders Bruce Breault and Tunny Ortali opened the original F. McLintocks in the fall of 1973. The business has grown to include five restaurants in Shell Beach, Pismo Beach, San Luis Obispo, Arroyo Grande and Paso Robles and now employs more than 400.

Current president Toney Breault likes to say that the first word he spoke was "beef." He was only two when his father opened the first restaurant and he grew up in the business, holding many positions in the company, from washing dishes on up.

If you want to take the experience home, many of the sauces and spices used at the restaurant are available in the big, friendly mercantile, and also online at www.mclintocks.com. Some of the delicious products include: Real Cowboy Steak Sauce, Callente Cowboy Hot Sauce, Original BBQ Sauce, Trial Camp Beans, BBQ Chef Seasoning, Cowboy Mild & Medium Salsa and Trail Camp Chili Fixins.

An evening at McLintocks is more than a meal; it's a total experience, one that keeps diners coming back again and again.

— Michael Chatfield

93

BAILEYANA

Blending Old-World Tradition with 21st Century Technology

The historic 1909 Independence Schoolhouse — now home to Baileyana's tasting room—lies in stark contrast to its state-of-the-art, steel and glass winery. In the vintage schoolhouse, sampling Baileyana's old-world style wines, there's a sense of stepping back in time. The high-tech winery is firmly planted in the 21st Century. While the appearance and technology of the winery are all "today," the style of hand-making fine wines here is centuries old.

In the 1970s, Jack and Catharine Niven were the first to plant wine grapes in the Edna Valley. While Jack focused on building the highly-respected Paragon Vineyard, avid gardener Catharine plotted off a 3.5 acre vineyard in her front yard. In keeping with her philosophy of "being the best you can be in whatever you pursue," Catharine researched vineyard styles prevalent in California and in Europe's great wine growing regions. True to her character, she took the challenging route, opting for vineyards more similar to those in

France's Burgundy region. Establishing Baileyana Winery, Catharine became one of the first women in the U.S. to own a wine label. Her passion for life and her philosophy remain the heart and soul of Baileyana to this day.

"She loved to zig when everyone else was zagging," says Baileyana's Director of Sales and Marketing John Niven of his grandmother. "She shrugged off the 'standard' methods of California viticulture of the time and adopted a Burgundian vineyard style — with tighter vine spacing and a more vertical approach to growing the vines."

Fueled by decades of experience and a passion for winegrowing, the Nivens purchased vacant land in the mid-1990s and planted what is now the Firepeak Vineyard. Close to the ocean, about four miles as the fog drifts, the vineyard nuzzles up to one of seven volcanic peaks known as "The Seven Sisters." Soil composed of marine sediment, sand, clay loam and volcanic rock —"dirt of the devil"— contributes to the intense varietal characteristics found in

Baileyana's Firepeak Vineyard wines. The Edna Valley is one of a handful of AVAs that enjoy the cooling ocean influences that promote a long ripening season and late harvest, creating exceptional depth of flavor in the Chardonnay, Pinot Noir, Sauvignon Blanc and Syrah grapes.

Not long after the Firepeak Vineyard was planted, Burgundy-born and - educated wine-maker Christian Roguenant was presented with an opportunity to create Burgundian style Chardonnay and Pinot Noir as well as old-world inspired Syrah and Sauvignon Blanc. Growing up among the vines, Christian studied enology and winemaking at the University of Dijon. A purist when it comes to winemaking styles, he learned to make Chardonnay and Pinot Noir in Burgundy, Sauvignon Blanc in Sancerre and New Zealand, Syrah in the northern Rhone region and Champagne at France's Champagne Deutz.

"This vineyard and the winery allow me to achieve my goal of making wine as true to the varietal as possible," say Roguenant. "I view the grapes as diamonds I am given by the growers. My job is to polish them to make better wine every year."

Catharine would be proud that her commitment to "being the best" has become a family tradition that enriches the tables, and lives, of wine lovers today.   — Melanie Bellon Chatfield

CONTRIBUTOR CONTACT INFORMATION

Baileyana
5828 Orcutt Road
San Luis Obispo, CA 93401
805.269.8200
805.269.8201 fax
www.baileyana.com
Tasting: 10am–5pm daily
Picnic Area

Baileyana is currently run by the third generation of the Niven Family who were among the early pioneers of the first vineyards planted in the Edna Valley. Knowledge gained from 30 years of farming our estate vineyards enables us to craft wines which embrace the union of viticulture, winemaking and terroir expression at its finest.

We invite you to visit our tasting room located in the historic Independence Schoolhouse. Try our award winning Pinot Noir, Chardonnay, Syrah and Sauvignon Blanc, as well as our limited production of Firepeak Vineyard designate wines.

98

Buona Tavola Ristorante
1037 Monterey St.
San Luis Obispo, CA 93401
805.545-8000

943 Spring St.
Paso Robles, CA 93446
805.237.0600

Opened in 1992, Buona Tavola (meaning "good table") is the realization of a dream. Working as an apprentice in the restaurants of his native Northern Italy, Antonio continued his training in Europe's finest hotels. He honed his skills on the Princess Cruise lines, and as executive chef in several award-winning Los Angeles eateries. Buona Tavola in downtown San Luis Obispo opened to rave reviews. The esteemed Zagat Survey gave it the highest ratings of any restaurant in the county, calling it "superb dining" with "great wine" in a "charming setting… one of the best between Los Angeles and San Francisco".

Claiborne & Churchill
2649 Carpenter Canyon Road
San Luis Obispo, CA 93401
805.544.4066
805.544.7012 fax
www.claibornechurchill.com
Tasting: 11am–5pm daily
Picnic Area; Special Events

Founded in 1983 by Claiborne (Clay) Thompson and Fredericka Churchill Thompson, this small family winery specializes in stylish and fruity dry wines made from Riesling, Gewürztraminer, Muscat, Pinot Gris, and Chardonnay grapes. Claiborne & Churchill's red wine is an elegant and flavorful Pinot Noir. A number of sweet dessert wines are also produced.

We encourage you to visit us in our eco-friendly "straw-bale" winery building, the first of its kind. We are located on Highway 227 in the Edna Valley, a few miles south of San Luis Obispo.

Eberle Winery

Eberle Winery
P.O. Box 2459
Paso Robles, CA 93447
805. 238.9607
805.237.0344 fax
www.eberlewinery.com
Tasting: 10 am - 5 pm Winter
10 am - 6 pm Summer

Celebrating 25 years of fine wine-making, Gary Eberle was one of the first to the region, pioneering one of California's premium wine producing appellations. From monthly Guest Chefs, reserve tastings, medal-winning new releases, to dinner and dancing under the stars, the casual elegance at Eberle is sure to make memories last a lifetime. Visit our 16,000 square feet of underground caves or take part in select VIP tours that Wine Spectator calls "One of the best tours on the Central Coast." Children and pets are always welcome. Private catered lunches, dinners & receptions are available in our Wild Boar Room or on our deck overlooking the beautiful Estate vineyards. Located on Hwy 46 East, 3.5 miles east of Hwy 101, Paso Robles.

EBERLE WINERY

EOS Estate Winery

EOS Estate Winery
5625 Highway 46 East
Paso Robles, CA 93446
805.239.2562
805.239.2317 fax
www.eosvintage.com
Daily: 10 am-5 pm
Summer/Weekends: 10 am -6 pm
Picnic Area; Special Events; Race Car Exhibit

Located in the premier winegrowing region of Paso Robles, the EOS Estate Winery has become a leading producer of award-winning varietal wines and a premier destination spot for travelers. The spectacular 104,000 square foot Romanesque facility was modeled after an Italian monastery, and is surrounded by 700 acres of beautiful estate vineyards. Visitors can enjoy old world ambiance while surveying the unique, carefully selected collection of fine wines, gourmet foods, and exquisite gifts. Beyond the tasting room there are lovely rose gardens, and lush picnic areas to explore, as well as informative, self-guided tours of the winery.

Hunt Cellars

Hunt Cellars
2875 Oakdale Road
Paso Robles, CA 93446
805.237.1600
www.huntcellars.com

Daily: 10:30am - 5:30pm

Driving along the scenic Highway 46 West, about three miles west of the 101 Hwy at Oakdale Road, you will find the dream that has become reality for David Hunt, Winemaker and owner of Hunt Cellars, a winery committed to producing "Memorable Wines". We believe that great wines leave indelible impressions when poured with wonderful meals and great friends and scintillating conversations. Hunt Cellars was founded on the philosophy of producing wines that you will look forward to simply sipping by a cozy fireplace or pairing with your favorite meals to enhance that special event or moment in time.

99

J. Lohr Vineyards & Wines

1000 Lenzen Avenue
San Jose, CA 95126
408.288.5057
408.293.1345 fax

6169 Airport Blvd.
Paso Robles, CA 93446
805.239.8900
805.239.0365 fax
www.jlohr.com
Tasting: 10am-5pm daily
Picnic Area in Paso Robles only, special
events in San Jose and Paso Robles

Celebrating 30 years of estate grown wines
of extraordinary quality, J. Lohr
Vineyards & Wines helped pioneer both
the Paso Robles appellation in San Luis
Obispo County — as well as the Arroyo
Seco appellation in Monterey County — as
premier winegrowing regions. Today, J.
Lohr owns and manages 2,000 and 900
vineyard acres respectively, focusing on
practices and techniques that showcase the
best flavors in its Valdiguié, Pinot Noir,
Syrah, Zinfandel, Cabernet Sauvignon
and Merlot red wines, and its Sauvignon
Blanc, Chardonnay, White Riesling and
White Zinfandel white wines.

Laetitia Vineyard & Winery

453 Laetitia Vineyard Drive
(directly off Highway 101)
Arroyo Grande, CA 93420
805.481.1772
805.481.6920 fax
www.laetitiawine.com

Situated in the Arroyo Grande Valley
of southern San Luis Obispo County,
Laetitia Vineyard & Winery is
dedicated to producing world-class
Burgundian-style wines with a special
focus on Pinot Noir. Our winery is
also noted for its production of French
inspired Methode Champenoise
sparkling wines. From a hillside
setting just 4 miles from the Pacific,
our vineyards enjoy cool sea breezes,
afternoon sun and a long growing
season. Our tasting room is open daily
from 11am to 5pm, sampling a
selection of both our Laetitia and
Barnwood Vineyard wines.

Mastantuono Winery

2720 Oak View Road
Templeton, CA 93465
805.238.0676
805.238.9257 fax
www.mastantuonowinery.com
Tasting Room: 10am-5pm daily
Picnic Area, Special Events

Located in the heart of Paso Robles
wine country, Mastantuono Winery
has specialized in producing fun,
approachable wines since 1976.
Visitors to our beautiful tasting room
can sample a wide array of white and
red wines, including many Italian
favorites, and two sparkling wines.
Our lovely grounds include a gazebo
picnic area and an Italian classic: the
Bocci Ball Court. We produce Chardonnay,
Chenin Blanc, White Zinfandel,
Muscat Canelli, Champagne, Raspberry
Champagne, Barbera, Carminello,
Cabernet Sauvignon, Sangiovese, Syrah,
Zinfandel, Merlot, and a Barbera-based
Port.

F. McLintocks Saloon & Dining House

750 Mattie Road
Shell Beach, CA 93449
800.866.6372
805.773.3050
805.773.5183 fax
www.mclintocks.com

Taste the Great American West

In an ocean-view setting right on Highway 101, F.McLintocks Saloon & Dining House offers the best in authentic ranch-style cooking and atmosphere teamed up with high-spirited customer service, world famous high-water pours, Award winning steaks and genuine western hospitality. Legendary oak-pit barbecued steaks and ribs are the finest, but seafood and salads are a specialty too.

Mon - Thurs 4:30pm - 9:30pm
Fri 4:00pm - 10:00pm
Sat 3:00pm - 10:30pm
Sun 4:00pm - 9:30pm
Early Bird Special Nightly!

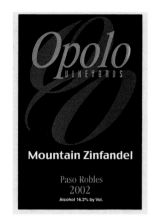

Opolo Vineyards

7110 Vineyard Drive
Paso Robles, CA 93446
805.238.9593
805.371.0102 fax
www.opolo.com
Tasting Room: 11am-5pm daily

Discover Opolo Vineyards, tucked out of sight just off Vineyard Drive on a rustic road that takes you through our estate vineyards, past owl boxes, oak trees, and a meandering creek, before arriving at the winery.

Expect to find "well extracted" wines with an explosion of forward fruit. That's what owners Rick and Dave enjoy, and with their 270 acres of vineyards on both the East and West side of Paso Robles, Opolo Vineyards is uniquely positioned to produce the finest ultra-premium wines.

Rancho Arroyo Grande Winery & Vineyards

591 Hi Mountain Road
Arroyo Grande, CA 93420
805.474.0220
805.474.0330 fax
www.ranchoarroyograndewines.com

First established as a Spanish land grant over 200 years ago, the time honored ways of the American West have always defined Rancho Arroyo Grande. The historic, 4,000 acre ranch is located in the picturesque Arroyo Grande Valley. Our 265 acres of vineyards are situated on hillsides, sloping plains, and on remote plateaus-each with a distinctive microclimate and soil.

In the vineyard and winery, we work tirelessly to farm the finest fruit and handcraft our wines to reflect the essence of this extraordinary land – specializing in Zinfandel and Rhone style wines.

SUMMERWOOD
W I N E R Y & I N N

Summerwood Winery & Inn

2175 Arbor Road
Paso Robles, CA 93446
805.227.1365 Winery
805.227.1111 Inn
www.summerwoodwine.com

We invite you to enjoy Summerwood wines at our relaxing tasting room and stay at our luxurious Four-Diamond inn. Summerwood is located in the heart of the Templeton Gap in beautiful Westside Paso Robles. Our focus is to produce the finest premium wines possible. Summerwood wines are available for sale exclusively in our tasting room and on our website.

Members of the Summerwood Seasons Club receive special pricing and VIP opportunities. Visit us online to join.

Vista Del Rey Vineyards

7340 Drake Road
Paso Robles, CA 93446
805.467.2138
805.467.2765 fax

Tasting: Most Sundays 11am-5pm and by appointment.
Picnic Area; Special Events

Vista Del Rey Vineyards is located six miles north of Paso Robles. Experience the many styles of Zinfandel, Barbera and more, while enjoying the panoramic view of the Santa Lucia Mountains from our acclaimed dry farmed vineyard. Limited rainfall and our silty-clay loam vineyards promote rich, fruit forward, food friendly wines. Since each growing season is different, each of our Estate wines offers a unique tasting experience.

Wild Horse Winery & Vineyards

1437 Wild Horse Winery Court
P.O. Box 910
Templeton, CA 93465
805-434-2541
www.wildhorsewinery.com
Picnic Area; Special Events

In twenty short years, Wild Horse Winery & Vineyards has grown from its humble beginnings to take its place as one of the Central Coast's leading producers of premium varietal wines. Located in the Paso Robles appellation, Wild Horse Winery was named for the wild mustangs that roam the hills and plains east of the vineyard estate. Experimentation, consumer education, environmental preservation, a sense of humor - these are the winery's core values. Today, the name Wild Horse is synonymous with quality and with world-class Pinot Noir, the winery's flagship varietal.

Paso Robles Vintners & Growers Association
P.O. Box 324
Paso Robles, CA 93447
805.239.8463
805.237.6439 fax
www.pasowine.com

Paso Robles Wine Country is located halfway between Monterey and Santa Barbara, on California's Central Coast. With a greater day-to-night temperature swing than any other appellation in California, Paso Robles Wine Country vines produce concentrated, yet balanced wines with intense varietal flavors. Paso Robles Wine Country's 75+ wineries offer world-class wines in every varietal, created by winemakers with diverse international influences.

San Luis Obispo Vintners & Growers Association
5828 Orcutt Road
San Luis Obispo, CA 93401
805.541.5868
805.541.3934 fax
info@slowine.com
www.slowine.com

Taste The Beauty! This cool climate viticultural area is located halfway between San Francisco and Los Angeles in South San Luis Obispo County. It is comprised of east/west running temperate valleys that open up to the ocean's influence including Edna Valley, Arroyo Grande Valley, Avila Valley and the Nipomo Mesa. The world-class micro climates and soils produce predominately Burgundian and Rhone varieties that have earned worldwide recognition and respect for their exceptional quality.

PHOTOGRAPHY CREDITS

Special thanks to the many local and regional photographers that contributed to this book, including: Wayne Holden, Wayne Capili, Margaretha Maryk

AUTHORS CREDITS

Melanie and Michael Chatfield are freelance writers who live and work in Hollister, California.

ORDERING INFORMATION

For more information about *WineStyle Paso Robles Wine Country • San Luis Obispo Wine Country* or *WineStyle Monterey County*, please visit **www.baypublishing.com** or call **831.373.8949**, Monday through Friday. You may also submit your requests by mail addressed to:

Bay Publishing Company
395 Del Monte Center, #103
Monterey, CA 93940
Fax 831.373.0290
Email: nancy@baypublishing.com